Tools for Sanity

Freedom, Peace, and Fulfillment in Every Moment

Kiran, Mystic girl in the City

·

ISBN 13: 9780615880969
ISBN: 0615880967
Library of Congress Control Number: 2013917351
Mystic Girl in the City, Felton, CA

For Christopher

You are home.
You are home already.
Home, where you are safe to rest and be exactly yourself . . .
No need to strive for success or fall into failure.
Just simply stop and take a breath and be yourself fully.
Rest in this moment, safe and unbound.

CONTENTS

Introduction: Waking Up

The stillness, the spaciousness . . .

That day about seven years ago, when I "woke up," what it actually felt like was that my mind blew a fuse. It got really quiet. And things that, until that exact moment, had shape and meaning became space. Empty space.

Instead of seeing a wall, for instance, all I could see was spaciousness, and a choice. I could only see a choice to see all this space as a "wall." I could feel a deep collective history of choice that this particular space will be seen as "wall."

You know how in grade 6 or 7 we learn that everything is actually made up of atoms? An atom is made of an electron that circulates around a neutron, magnetically drawn to the proton inside, and everything is made up of these atoms moving through space. Things only appear to be a wall or a table, but actually are made up of vast space filled with moving atoms. Well, when my mind blew, I could see from the perspective of atoms. I could see the space inside the walls and tables. Things began to appear more quantum to me, more as choices, as potential—potential energy, spaciousness that comes into form.

I literally became primarily identified as the vast space that is every *thing's* essence. More accurately, I became disidentified as me, this person, this personality, this body, this mind, this human. I dissolved and became space. Space replaced my identity; space became my foreground, and my essential being. The filter that turns the vast space of the universe into forms, like walls and tables and such, was not in operation. My mind blew a fuse. No better way to know what exactly "mind" is than to have it suddenly shut off. Without the filter of the mind . . . space. All form is seen as its primary source: space.

And I noticed that space has movement. Space moves. The movement feels like love. It is love. At the quantum level, love is what is created when space, the source of all forms, moves. The electron is magnetically attracted to the proton . . . love.

And love too has movement; love moves. That movement becomes what we feel and know as creativity, as desire. All the forms of our universe, from tiny atoms to massive galaxies, are sourced from space, a space that moves as love, as creativity, and eventually comes into what we see and experience as form. A wall, a table, but also thoughts, sensations, feelings, ideas, words—these are all forms. Forms of space.

And, curiously, all this space is aware. Aware of itself. There is not something that is aware of space; there is only space aware of space. Nothing separate from itself; the heart of all forms noticing itself. Space is aware.

Weird.

My experience of being "awake" simply means awareness is primarily aware of itself as space first, and identifies as form as a very distant second. Not as a mental construct or idea, but directly. No mind. No allegiance to form, nothing.

And that can be felt, more than known with the mind. Awareness is aware of itself, which is why some teachers say enlightenment is "self-authenticating." It's odd, but it knows itself intimately. Awareness knows if it's "awake," knows if it's "asleep"—that is, primarily identified as form, a person, a body, a mind, a history, and so on. There is just one thing here: space. And space is aware.

For some time, all the forms that are shaped out of space were very much in the background and could hardly be seen as distinct from space. So, my mind blew a fuse, and it kind of made it hard to get around, but there you go. It's an odd thing. A very odd thing to have your mind spontaneously blow.

No Context, No Devotion

I was never a spiritual person. I used to like conversations about there being more to us than meets the eye, but that was pretty much the extent of it. I had a copy of Seth Speaks, taken from my mom's bookcase, that I kinda tried to read. I loved nature, I loved rocks and their crystalline nature, and riverbeds full of dragon eggs. I loved aboriginal cultures of the world. I did yoga for fitness and usually skipped the "breathing stuff." As a child, New Age conversations were fun and interesting, but so were bike rides, and apple crisp just the way my mom makes it. I loved to talk about psychological things. But I was not raised to have any religious affiliations, and I had no devotion to any spiritual practice, no conversations about historical or contemporary enlightenment or awakening. I'd never really heard of anything like that. I was deeply involved in my artistic career. And I was deeply devoted to finding a way to heal from a very violent past that left me with a severe case of post-traumatic stress disorder.

I was a professional artist. A creator. I created original dance and theatre performances for my own arts company, and I toured as an independent actor and dancer. This was the practice in my life. I studied fine arts at university and had a fifteen-year professional practice, before the whole mind-blowing-up thing.

Regardless of my lack of any real spiritual awareness, one day, after lunch with my mom and her twin sister, and en route to meeting a friend . . . I died. In my bedroom: changing shoes one moment, dead the next. At first there was a strange noticing that my body was really very beautiful, really made of light . . . and then, poof! All form gone. All space. No form. Form was gone.

I did not have any words to describe what had happened. I had watched a comedy routine a few weeks back that my roommate and I were particularly tickled by. It was a sketch about "rapture insurance," the punchline being that you should get insurance in case you suddenly disappear. So that was the word I used: *raptured*. "I raptured." And that was the beginning of the wildest, most painful, and most beautiful ride. Not only did the mind blow up, leaving only space, but space has become more and more rich and full, and unfathomably detailed, as the years go by.

There was this one day, a few months later, once form started coming somewhat back into focus, where I could see both the form and the space. Space—in its true essence, pure space—and as its manifest essence, forms. It was a part of the integration process. And for a while, especially that day years ago, they were both meeting in the middle, neither more dominant than the other.

It was like this: I had to go to the train station to pick up my friend and her baby son. So I had to leave the apartment to take the elevator to the car park. But when I stepped into the elevator, I could not see the elevator so much; it was more an elevator shaped out of space—not only space, but also elevator, and not only elevator, but space. It was like *pretending* to step into the elevator—no me, no elevator, but still a me and an elevator and a timeline for an appointment . . . and no appointment, no time. I pushed the "button," essentially space, but I was aware of the *choice* for seeing buttons. It was so funny, hysterically funny. I know primarily there is no elevator, no me, no buttons to push. This elevator is not going anywhere, nobody is going anywhere. Nobody, going nowhere. But it appeared as an elevator carrying a woman, me, to the car park. Then I got to the "car" and apparently drove out into the street. It was pee-your-pants funny. There is no "driving," in the same way there is no elevator. Just an appearance of driving a car. And the best part was that it was a busy street, full of cars, full of nothing going nowhere, pretending to drive, captivated by an illusion that wasn't appearing as an illusion to me. Like the child who sees the emperor has no clothes.

It's so hard to put into words.

But remember those little stick drawings, where you draw a figure at the bottom corner of a book, and if you run the pages very fast through your fingers, it looks like your stick drawings are dancing or running or moving? And still you know it's just a stick drawing and it's not really alive and dancing? It was just like that. And the mind filters that drawing to look like movement. It seems like we are all "driving," moving, alive and dancing. But nobody is really driving; there is just space appearing and the illusion of this car, road, woman, world. And the mind is the part that filters it to appear real, to appear to move and be separate, and to have histories and stories.

But I didn't have a mind. It blew its fuse, and the filter was gone. Only the space was left, and its hinted shapes of a world. Nothing to make it appear real or to move it. And so, just space. Then eventually the choice of space, the choice of form, and a little filter—just enough of a filter so that this dream appeared in all the space . . . an elevator, a car park, a train station, an appointment, a friend, a baby. And still mostly nothing. So funny.

Illusion—literally living and moving and playing in an illusion.

A Fairly Extreme Nightmare

True story:

This awakening, this mind blowing a fuse, was so sudden, so completely out of the blue, that I had no orientation for this explosion, this death. This pure blast of unfiltered reality.

And so I went through a massive process of unwinding. If you can imagine, I was kinda still alive, but all my identity and history and stories were very suddenly and drastically being taken from me. It felt weirdly personal and incredibly scary, as though the "nothingness" was taking everything from me. A big nothingness was coming for me and stealing everything else . . . *everything*. Forever. That's what it felt like. I died very suddenly, but then death came back to slowly make sure there was nothing still standing. Unwinding any momentum of "me" that might habitually come back into form. Like the fan was unplugged, but each blade that still had momentum was being stopped.

It was months of living through death after dying. To be living through my own death. Fully dying, never again to have this life, to know myself as this woman, with this woman's memories, or dreams—all of it was being wiped out. I was being suddenly wiped out. Primarily a lot of pain and horror, that's how it felt. Like being buried alive, and slowly, powerlessly, aware that you are dying, but having to wait for all of your systems to shut down. Having to experience your survival instinct screaming, gasping for life, however impotently. A fairly extreme nightmare.

Of course, "I" was not being wiped out. It was my identities being wiped out. But until you die, you *are* those identities. As much as I grasped and resisted, the vast space, what actually felt like a void, was too powerful and was erasing "me" faster that I could hold on. All of me—all my concepts, my beliefs, and my most precious memories—were being drained of their life. It felt like everything was being eaten by the big nothing. And I couldn't save anything.

For all the glorious stories of a sudden awakening, all the wondrous fantasies some folks dream about, in reality, it's actually dying. Fully, completely dying. That's also included in my definition of awakening. I realize others have a bigger spectrum of definition that includes more subtle recognitions. But personally, I know if you're awake, because you died. And the dead have a unique feel about them. You don't have to be told; you know it.

(And I don't always recommend it. I don't think you have to die in order to be free. That's just how it happened for me.)

When I first came into contact with a very, very good spiritual teacher who was very capable of leading folks right to this doorway, I was about two months into this. And I was appalled by his teaching. I walked into a room and saw three hundred people listening to Adyashanti explain how it all is. And I wanted to throw rocks at him and scream for everyone to leave the room. I walked up to the microphone and yelled at him to stop . . . stop! I was certain that nobody in the room could understand the actual reality of this experience, the death. Nobody could possibly want the rug so thoroughly pulled out from under them. It was so awful to imagine that someone who came to listen to this guy speak, or because a friend said 'you have to hear this guy', or came for a nice evening of meditation away from the chaos of the kids at home, might unknowingly, suddenly, spontaneously die. Not metaphorically, because you are only metaphorically alive, but a real death. It was a nightmare. I didn't know these kinds of meetings happened. I didn't know about dharma talks and satsang and vipassana. And this teacher was—is—so good, so awake, and so articulate that it was excruciating to watch.

Since then we've become very good friends, and he tells me that he enjoyed my protest, and that he tells this story a lot.

If PTSD Was a Hard Storm, This Was the Tsunami

As you can imagine, dying in this way, for me, involved massive primal fear exploding. And uniquely for me, with all this fear came . . . well, a gift of sorts. I blew up so massively that I became a channel, a channel for much of the world's fear. Fear from throughout the ages came up to be rinsed free of identity, right through my body-mind.

Guess I'm just lucky that way.

It began a few weeks after the big mind blow. I was scheduled to be on a work trip in Edinburgh. Up until this point, I had just kind of continued on with my life, a very truncated version, a very strange and silent and still version of nothing: nothing going to work, nothing staring at the tree out of my window, "working." Needless to say, lots of sick days. And then this trip.

In hindsight, I knew the fear was coming. I could feel its movement for a few hours prior, at the airport, where I was having a hard time letting go of my friend Christopher's hand. When I had to go through security, I wanted to crawl back into his pocket and go home. He had to peel me off his body and literally push me through airport security.

A few hours after I landed in Edinburgh, the eruption happened. Looking back, apparently I had to be away from familiar ground. I needed to be without any support for this massive gripping fear to erupt. Now, in my previous life, as I mentioned, I suffered from post-traumatic stress disorder, so I was no stranger to paralyzing fear. But this was a whole different ball game. If PTSD was a hard storm, this was the tsunami. For those of you who know Edinburgh, I was staying in the "pubic triangle," a particular corner where three rather low-end strip clubs meet. Late at night the brawls start up, and the roaches come up for beer and blood and other grim bits. I had rented a rather nice apartment, not knowing the area, and the front window of the place faced this corner. About fifty minutes after I arrived at my flat, fear exploded. Fear from every lifetime, every storyline, from all time, erupted through my body-mind. Historical memories of men butchered at war and queens being executed, while violence erupted on the streets, literally: fistfights, screams, bugs coming out of the sidewalk, fists coming through the glass window of the apartment.

About twenty-seven hours later, I found myself on a street corner, shaking, holding a pay phone, Christopher on the line:

"Are you breathing?"

"Yes."

But not my finest moment. Big eyes of terror, holding that pay phone for dear life, shaking so badly I could barely stand. Christopher comforted me with images of how, in later days, they might tell this story in our language, the language of the stage:

"The stage is dark, and suddenly a small pool of light shines on a face, a woman's face, with big, scared eyes, for like two minutes . . . nothing but those eyes, and silence. Then she looks up at the audience and says . . . 'I just shit my pants.'"

Then Christopher said to come home.

Two days later, I simply collapsed in the middle of a busy Edinburgh street. A homeless man found me and eventually took me to the hospital. The doctors couldn't figure out what was wrong, and I didn't know how to say: *Fear. Terror. Death. I am consciously walking through my own death. I am dying alive. And all the fear and violence and pain of many lives, in many ages, is exploding through my being.* Seventeenth-century orphanages, ancient wars—the whole war, all of it. I was consciously walking through the heart of hell, and I could not keep it together. But a hospital is not really the best place to die alive, so I eventually came home.

There are so many illusions about enlightenment. So many stories of how it's all grace and bliss and heaven. Well, this is what it looks like sometimes, oftentimes. It's a horror show. A horror show at such a high level that only the dead can actually survive. After awakening to our true nature, many of us experience this unravelling of a dark, hellish pain, usually deeply unconscious, which often includes pain from larger cultural or global incidents stored in our cell memory. If you were suddenly forced to process it all with a fully operational mind, it would be unbearable. Imagine the pain most of us have to process regardless, just living our ordinary lives, living day to day in a society with abuse, rape, violence, war etc. Now multiply that intensity by 10,000—that's what it's like. Ultimately, this unravelling begins a process of profound healing, eventually giving way to a sweet and profound liberation.

Seeing the Code

So these days, years later, I still see primarily from the "quantum field," from the place of pure space and pure choice. It's hard to describe . . . I tell people I see the "code," where formlessness, or space, encodes to becomes form. Perhaps about 10 percent of my mind eventually came back; some days it feels like 20 percent. So it's weird to be me. I get lots and lots of information from this vantage point, at the level of code, and I somehow do okay, reading code to notice the form. I spent many years very overwhelmed by it all, but now it's mostly okay.

Human relationships are weird. I get a lot of information about the unconditioned "truth" arising for someone, but rarely do other humans listen or move from their "truth." Instead, they move from conditioned responses—conditioning from childhood, from mental lists of "shoulds"—which I cannot see, and know very little about. So, I almost never understand what anyone is doing. For example, I can feel, see, and know you're hungry, but I don't know why you're going to mow the lawn. I don't know why you're not eating something first. I can feel, see, and know that you're sad, but when I ask you how you are, you say you're fine and that everything is great. And if I say, "I was wondering if you're feeling sad," I hear, "Nope, I'm good." And, well, about a million more of these types of things, all day, every day. And it can be weird for folks to be with me too . . . it's kinda awkward when someone sees very clearly into your hidden or unconscious patterns, or your conditioned habits, especially if that's not an area you're wanting to deal with. It can feel humiliating and disempowering, or awesome and liberating, depending on the day or the mood. On the plus side, I can be a really great resource for seeing how to shift those patterns, because I can see right at the level of where they initiate. So, if you need some clarity, or just want some insight, there is a good chance I can help.

When I am coaching folks, I find that I'm usually guiding folks through these unconscious patterns, ultimately pointing out how the pain can transform into peace. I point out the pathway to what I call *sanity*. Sanity, to me, is living and moving from the pure impulse of authenticity. It's something unique to each individual, a unique blueprint of authentic, right action. And to this end, I notice that I keep pointing out some very basic and innate tools for the job. Four tools: Awareness, Acceptance, Alchemy, and Alignment.

Tools for Sanity

one

Awareness

Awareness is effortless. As effortless as breathing, as inseparable from you as your own breath. You can't be apart from awareness. In this moment, you're aware of these words, of the sounds in the room, of the feeling of air on your skin. There is always some awareness about you. That is the first tool for sanity, something so effortless and so readily available. Simply awareness.

A Constant Avoidance

All that you are, every bit of you—including the pain, including your struggles with life—is intelligent, is there for a very good reason. We usually can't access the reason; just the struggle, just the pain. And we are conditioned to work really hard to avoid this. We don't want to be aware of our struggles and pain. We don't want to look at the puppet master. For a lot of us, we just want out of this—we are seeking for something else, a different experience of life. We seek love, power, money, or enlightenment in order to change the current experience of struggle and pain and dissatisfaction. We don't want to be aware, acutely aware, of what is going on in this moment. We have an idea of awareness, or consciousness, as somewhere else, somewhere bliss-filled and without pain, struggle, bad behavior, failed relationships, failing health, and so on.

But awareness is here. Consciousness is here, when and where the pain meets you. Awareness is always aware, even when you are struggling. You can be aware of pain, and feel peace in doing it. Shocking news, I know. But most of us, if we get right down to the root of it, are actually longing to simply stop all the ferocious effort involved in living. What I see is that most of that effort is because of repression, or trying to get away from pain. And the effort includes some kind of avoidance of what is going on right here, right now. There can be such relief when we stop and simply become aware of what is really going on. It sounds like hell to the mind, but it actually feels very different.

There is a constant conditioned movement to avoid being aware, being aware right now. Especially to avoid seeing that there may be something very painful here. There is a profound pressure to be selective toward what you want to be "one" with, what you want to be "now" with. A deep habitual practice of separation to maintain a shield from that pain.

So I invite you to look very, very deeply at your propensity to ignore things. Your blindness. With compassion and with humor, notice how actively you ignore and shield; how we shield away from pain because it gets triggered by the world, and shield away from the world because it triggers our pain.

How profoundly we have sectioned ourselves off. Can you notice the barrier?

Imagine a wonderful lover. Imagine feeling such love towards them, but actually saying no every time they come around. Imagine you avoid them, hide from them, and generally just fantasize about your loving relationship with them, but refuse to actually spend much time with them. Imagine that you are very, very selective, very decided on what is okay to love and what is not. Very occasionally saying okay and being with them, but only when being with them looks and feels like this one specific way.

Can you feel how unfulfilling that relationship would be? How absent of the heat of love? How confusing for the lover? How impotent and filled with struggle and frustration?

This is how I hear many of you feel about your relationship with God, life, the infinite. I hear you say you are confused and sometimes feel so impotent. I hear you have lots of struggle. I hear you say you feel devoid of the heat of love. You feel left out.

Because, my friends, you don't notice the *no*. How often you say "no!"

So notice it. Just be aware of what you actively avoid.

I ask you to simply notice. Effortless, and innate to your being, is awareness. And there is great power in that simple awareness; there is a ton of juice in being aware. No action on your part is required. Awareness is required. Awareness takes care of itself. The first tool in the path back to freedom is awareness. Not action. It's awareness. Forced action does not actually get you very far on its own. Jumping into action as a primary tool is actually a very short-term solution. It just lops the head off the struggle for a moment, until your attention wanders and suddenly you're struggling again. Awareness is way less work than that, and way more permanent. We want to get to the root of where the insanity is happening, and to do that we need great big doses of awareness. The beautiful, effortless, totally available stuff.

To begin with, we have to start to notice the *no* and the very selective bits of Oneness we are willing to be okay with. It will be shocking to fully notice how much no is going down. Heck, I'm going to put a big wager on that! I'll wager that when you fully notice how contrary you have been to life, how fickle your part of the relationship with existence has been, things are going to make some sense about your journey.

And the point is, pain is the creator of your unsatisfactory, or downright painful, life experiences; and avoiding it only creates more of those experiences you're actively avoiding. Pain comes from a wound, a wound that is repressed, dense energy in your system. And this energy can release and heal. You are not separate from life, and life is a powerful healer and profound creator. Love or pain create all the forms of the universe. And in order to heal the pain, transforming it to love . . . well, the first part of this is awareness. Awareness of what you avoid, awareness of when you avoid, and awareness of what is really going on behind all that avoidance.

And this is such good news. Because you are capable of awareness. It takes more energy to be *unaware* than it takes to be aware. You have to actually create a block to awareness, because it's always effortlessly happening. No matter what. You are aware. It's so funny, because there you are, seeking for something, anything else. Looking away from what is actually right here, well within your ability. Seeking for joy and happiness, and truth and freedom and ease. And to embody these things, you have to start right here and right now. And it begins with being aware of the effort to not be here.

We Are Entranced

When source, stillness, spaciousness—take your pick—is moving, it can sometimes assume dense energetic forms, as a wound, as pain, some kind of pain in our system. We can feel this pain physically, emotionally, and mentally. That pain has a voice, a very aggressive loop in your head, and it tells us all kinds of scary things. It especially likes to tell us what is wrong with the world and is very aggressive with describing what is wrong with you. It tells graphic stories about what we "lack." Graphic and painful stories about a lack of love, a lack of joy or peace, or perhaps a lack of ability, or power, or freedom. And these painful stories are so constant and so convincing that we are entranced by them. Instead of looking at the voice itself—or its painful source, the dense, energetic, physical sensation in your system—we move toward seeking to fill this apparent lack, believing the story utterly and completely. Thus begins the constant seeking for joy, happiness, truth, and freedom, even though freedom is actually only ever right here, never far away.

When we look a little closer, we can see that seeking has not actually ended our pain. Not usually. And not permanently. And seeking can actually become a big part of the problem. The constant movement to seek becomes quite painful.

But seeking is also rather natural. Seeking is a necessary part of what we may call evolution, a natural human impulse to seek in order to grow and change. We seek God, we seek love, we seek money, we seek power, we seek intimacy and connection, on and on. Follow any forty-eight hours of any of us, awakened or not, and you will see each of these cycles playing out. But when fueled by pain, by the constant loop in your head about "what you lack," the seeking becomes more acute and much more painful.

Let's try something . . .

You know that thing you want so bad?

Perhaps it's the one thing you want most in the world. The thing you find yourself unconsciously seeking in almost every moment. Freedom or enlightenment? Perhaps love? Perhaps never having to worry about money? Or never suffering physical pain? Or all of the above? Really, what is the one thing that, no matter what you do, you just can't seem to get fulfilled? No matter how many books, or interviews, or courses you invest in, what is that elusive goal, that thing that seems to constantly ache, but is always out of reach?

Now feel into your body, see if there is an ache, or a throbbing sensation, perhaps in your heart or gut? There is a dense wound, a pain repressed deep in your system. Can you notice it? It has a physical sensation, and an emotional emanation, and an aggressive thought loop. That is what is emanating your story about lack, even though it seems like its your experience of lack that is creating the story. The loop in your head tells a graphic and painful story. That story rolling around 24/7 then creates your experience of lack. That is the real reason you experience the lack: because of the constant story. Not the other way around. In reality—actual reality—you're not capable of lacking anything.

It's not experience that creates the story; it's the story that creates the experience.

And that story also creates your growing desperation, or "grasp."

One major reason you can't ever feel the fulfillment of this particular desire is because of this deep grasp. The deep tension is actually what keeps what you want from being experienced, because similar to how the same charge on the ends of a magnet—positive and positive— repel each other, the grasp is repelling your fulfillment. The grasp, on a quantum level, is actually a positive energetic force. And the underlying natural desire is also a positive energetic charge. A positive force meeting another positive will repel each other. So the grasp is adding this extra repelling positive charge.

Letting go of the grasp releases the extra positive charge. This leaves the desire, or natural impulse of seeking— a positive energetic charge—to move simply toward "having," a negative energetic charge. Seeking and having are magnetically attracted to each other. Positive attracts negative. Just as electrons are magnetically attracted to protons inside the atoms that make up all the forms of the universe. That's how it moves around here.

When we move without a painful story, when there are no wounds in the system projecting these painful mental loops, there is no desperation and grasp, no added charge. And such desires usually come into form quickly. We have all experienced it, like when you are thinking of someone, and suddenly they call you. That is a desire without any lack story, no woundedness around it; and rather quickly, it takes form. We all have many experiences like this all the time. Watch and you'll notice: all day long your natural impulse of seeking becomes having rather quickly.

But those desires that feel desperate have a large charge, or grasp, on them, meaning they are fueled by pain in your system. Meaning they have an extra charge and therefore can't be fulfilled until that extra charge is released. Basically, they need some more support. The grasp needs to be unhooked.

But how do you do this? How exactly do you unhook a desperate, painful grasp? Ultimately, the answer is in healing the dense, stuck energy in your system. The full answer is in healing the wound that is unconsciously spinning the painful mental loop in your head, and convincing you that you are less than, worthless, separate, and so on.

But the shortcut, and first major step, is awareness.

You need awareness to let it go. How many times have you tried and tried and tried to let something go, and it hasn't worked? It hasn't worked because of a dense system of pain undermining your attempts. But what will work is awareness. Awareness is like seeing the power source, and unplugging it. And to unplug the power, you have to be aware—really, really aware of what is going on.

The power source fueling the grasp is that wound, that repressed pain in your system. There will be an armoring around this raw, repressed pain. This armoring is sometimes called *ego*, the story of a me that is separate and has to struggle in life to get its needs met. The repressed wound and the armor need to be seen, really seen to be unplugged. Luckily, awareness is how we begin to unplug the power fueling it all. And awareness is effortless!

No wound or power behind it all, no constant story of lack.

No constant story of lack, no desperate experience of lack.

No desperate experience of lack, no grasping.

No grasping, no extra positive charge.

No extra positive charge, instant manifestation. (or law of attraction, or "it just all worked out beautifully, even better than I expected.")

So, let's find the pain, the ego, and the lacking story. Let's see what is going on . . .

Try this: What is the worst-case scenario? What is the worst thing that can happen if you don't get that thing? If you never taste God ? Not one drop of bliss? Or say you never find that true love, or you never make that money? What's the worst? Absolute worst?

Now look . . . really, really deeply . . . WHO is actually harmed if this worst-case scenario unfolds?

Is the vast stillness of all life going to have a problem if it never gets enlightened?

No, stillness itself is not trying to get anywhere. Certainly not trying to get enlightened.

Is God going to die if it never wakes up to truth?

God is truth. Again . . . not looking. Truth is not going to die, ever.

Is love going to kill itself if it never falls in love again and is all alone forever with ten cats?

No, love is doing fine. Love doesn't ever need to "fall in love"; love is already in love. No falling needed. Love itself does not need to get anywhere. Nope, it's not love that is seeking.

So who—who needs to fall in love? Who needs to get enlightened, who needs to make more money, have more power? Who needs to be free? Me? Who is me?

My wager: the lack story. The story that you are out of love, separate from God, without worth, imprisoned— that story is the only thing trying to get back to love. You, you're here already. You're the one noticing that painful desperation; you're the one noticing the pain. And because of my particular point of view, I can see very clearly that you are the vast awareness that is aware of the pain.

You're just caught. You're captivated by the 24/7 loop and are very quickly identified with it. A quick slip and you don't notice that, in fact, you are the one here that is noticing the 24/7 loop, noticing the desperation, noticing the pain, and therefore you can't be the loop, the desperation, or the pain. Are you the noticing? Or the experience?

I know it usually feels like you are the experience, but you wouldn't notice that pain if you were the pain. You can't be pain and be the awareness of pain. You're the one who is in pain. More correctly, the pain is in you.

Pain, wounds, egoic beliefs all eclipse the basic truth that you're the one noticing it. You're the awareness. When you stop looking at your life from this mental loop, you see from awareness itself. Look directly at awareness. That's you.

Obviously, right? The awareness came first. But you get caught not noticing this because of some deep wounds generating a very constant, tenacious, and loud loop of thoughts. Very captivating, very trance-inducing.

Regardless, is awareness going to suffer if it doesn't get enlightened (or doesn't get that dream house, or dream bank account, or perfect loving relationship)? Nope.

Nope.

The only one who is going to hurt is the ego, the lack story. That which is hurting to begin with because it is sourced from pain. That is why you feel pain; not because you are lacking and need to become fulfilled, but because pain itself is what is fueling this whole goose chase! Pain is what is causing the grasping. Grasping is what is creating the massive tension. So, it's not about seeking. (Personally I think seeking is fine, desire is fine, wishes are fine—especially if they are such a deep, aligned, full-of-life and pulsating yummy yes.) It's about seeing what is really going on here. It's about becoming aware of the the grasp, the repelling force, keeping the natural and effortless manifestation out of reach.

See the devil behind it all. To unhook the grasp, you need to truly see it. So let's apply all that effortless awareness, that effortless awareness that is reading these words, to notice all the details about the mental loop, the emotional field, and the repressed wound. When you see it, bring lots of awareness. You will not be so easily fooled again, so quickly captivated and convinced that you're the pain and need to find love or God or power to be fulfilled. That is the magnificent power of awareness: once something is fully, truly seen, it can't ever be unseen. It's like turning on the lights in a dark room. When the room is dark, you bump into things; once you turn on those lights, you see perhaps there is a table and couch in the room, maybe a little toy fire truck on the floor. Even if it gets dark again, you know what's there. You're not going to unsee the table or couch or toy because the lights go out again. Unless you were only glancing . . .not really being aware. If you only take a quick glance, you may actually step into the room and right on to that toy truck.

However, once the lights are on. . . once you see this painful story, the emotional field, the repressed wound, once you notice that you're the awareness, not the desperation. . . then, when you are caught in tremendous pain again, and under the spell of the terrific story again, you'll better understand what's actually going on.

I don't mean knowing all this intellectually, or hearing me tell you it, or reading all about it. Actually take a deep look yourself. Directly experience this yourself. Go on, take a look. I mean it, put this book down and try it out.

Actually see for yourself the details in the lack story, the typical storylines, and the pain. Notice that you don't have to avoid it or block it out, that it's truly less effort to simply see it, rather than continue to repress it, and flail in such continual pain. See what "it" is. That's where, and how, the grasp begins the real and permanent process of letting go.

Amber: Is Amber Awareness?

Amber: *I have had lots of experience noticing what I call "the everything." I have these glimpses of openings and bliss. Sometimes it feels like "nothingness" too. I have had these glimpses since I was a child. I get these glimpses, but in my concepts, I think there should be more, like a deep realization. I feel like I am missing out.*

Kiran: What happens when you are not having "glimpses"?

I shrink back into myself, and I get focused in my mind, in my work. I guess I need to focus more on awareness, but I focus on my mind, and life.

So in those times when you glimpse that there is nothing . . . are you there?

When I experience those glimpses . . . there is a body, and talking, and, well . . . I guess there is no Amber. Unless I think of it.

Is Amber being nothing, or is nothing happening?

Nothing is happening.

However, when you are captivated by the mind and focused on work, and life, being Amber, you think that Amber needs to be awareness. So, Amber thinks she has to do something to be awareness. There is a hook there. There is a story, that "Amber can't be awareness because 'awareness doesn't work,' 'doesn't do life,' 'doesn't sit at a desk,' 'doesn't suffer bosses.'"

Amber feels like a superimposition on nothingness.

Yes, but it's nothingness doing that.

It's nothing imposing on nothing?

Could it be Amber?

No . . . how could it be Amber?

Does Amber have the power to be Infinity?

No.

Does infinity have the power to be Amber?

Yes . . . if it wanted to, it sure could!

I would say that's what it is doing. Nothing seems to be coming into form as Amber. It's not Amber doing it, right?

Right.

So, maybe nothing is being Amber.

Yes.

I would agree, nothing seems to be coming into form, having a personality, having a body, and that personality/body is what we are calling Amber, and this includes having a job, making dinner, feeding the kids. It's not Amber doing it.

When it's all going on it seems like Amber. Right. Wow. I can see this. It's easy. It's not some huge herculean effort to see all this.

Yes. Your whole life has been nothing coming into form, a form we are calling Amber. That is a big part of my job, to point out what you already know, because it's so easy to miss. You've been it your whole life! You have been aware of this since you were a child, that you are the awareness, not the objects in awareness, but it's very easy to miss.

two

Acceptance

Sometimes you just get tired. Tired of trying to improve, trying to get somewhere, of trying to heal, or be better or be in less pain, or be enlightened. Techniques, strategies, practices become too much. And when we simply can't run toward or away from anything anymore, we stop and finally, finally just say okay. Yes. This is it. This is me, this is pain, this is hurt, this is enough, this is frustrating, this is fatigue. Just yes. Simply yes. That is acceptance. And that is a primary tool of sanity. No more getting away from, no more trying to get somewhere, just finally saying yup, yup, this is where I am.

And you don't have to get tired. Instead of waiting for the exhaustion you can just say okay, yes as soon as you notice something. Yes is always *present, acceptance is always available to you. A simple willingness. I promise, It's always here.*

Do You Really Want the Truth?

As I mentioned, I'm not very spiritual. I just don't know much about it. I don't know what a noble truth is, or what advaita means, or what a sutra is. Forgive my ignorance. For this argument, my distance may provide some insight.

It seems a lot of folks pursue spirituality as a way to find something more, something that will uplift their experience. Perhaps because of suffering and a desire to heal it, or understand it, or change it. Or as a way to find freedom or more fulfillment. So sane!

But there is something I want to point out. There seems to be a simple misunderstanding that mistakes feeling happy for being free and fulfilled. For instance, the mind habitually categorizes experience into good and bad. On the good side, we have peace, love, kindness, forgiveness, patience and so on. On the bad side, anger, rage, jealousy, frustration, resentment, impatience, etc. We could say its like a filter. "This rainy day is wonderful, we can hear the rain on the roof!" Or, "This rainy day sucks . . . nothing but rain and more rain!" And in spirituality, we often harbor the belief that the only things worth experiencing are those the mind categorizes as good. And basically what I see is that this creates a simple misunderstanding: our focus is placed on taking whatever shows up—for example, an emotion—and shaping it into something else, making it something that fits the category of "good."

Now, awake people don't tend to do this. Instead, there is a simple embrace of what is.

There are some personalities of awake folks that rejoice in whatever shows up; some personalities have no bias whatsoever for what's showing up; and some personalities rejoice when what is happening feels like joy and rage when what is happening feels like rage. But there is little to no movement to change what is arising. I am speaking primarily of what is arising inside of you, not outside. It's all inside anyway, but let's say *inside* —the emotions and what it feels like inside your body.

So, for instance, let's say you paid a huge amount of money for an amazing night at a swanky hotel, and you get there and it's a smoky-smelling room, the size of a closet, with stale bed sheets, facing a loud highway. And a few thick, curly hairs right in the middle of the pillowcase.

A person who is clear or awake in that moment will likely just accept feeling frustration, anger, regret, etc; notice the emotions arising, welcome them, discern if it's appropriate to express them, perhaps yes, perhaps no. But there is no repression. This is not a mind-managed process, it's not a mindfulness practice, it's an acceptance. A welcome of simple emotions versus a rejection or a judgment, or a management, etc. Then, an attending to what these emotions need, ie) an apology and some kind of action from the hotel staff, or to leave and find another place to stay or whatever, but some kind of full acceptance and attendance.

Someone coming from a spiritual misunderstanding will habitually or unconsciously judge the emotions they are having. They may feel like there is something wrong with a negative feeling, and try to repress it, to instead "look for the lesson" in the situation, or look for some good qualities within the events. Or there can be some kind of management program to acknowledge the emotions but then bypass any negative feelings. And sometimes, we can simply not even be aware of our negative feelings, being so practiced at finding a fast resolve to "happy"—the best of the "good" qualities. Regardless, there is no warm welcome, no acceptance, no honest willingness to simply allow yourself to feel whatever you are feeling.

Basically it could all just come down to this:

Do you simply just want to feel happy?

Or do you want something deeper? Do you want Freedom? Fulfillment?

You will know what you want more.

If what you really want is to feel happy, you will notice that many, many times in a day, you will feel happy. You will find that you collapse and root out any emotions or qualities that don't feel happy, and align with the "happier" emotions. You will primarily notice happiness and avoid the rest until happiness becomes your major operating system.

If what you really want is freedom, then you want the truth, which is freedom. You will notice that many, many times in a day, you get the truth. You refuse to avoid, you refuse to repress; instead, you're aware, you welcome and fully accept. Because what you really want is the truth. That's where freedom is. You can feel it. Truth, freedom, fulfillment. And each truth does collapse on itself until eventually you will hit ground on the final truth.

Do you want to be free? Then you want the truth. You will pick truth no matter what.

I make it sound simple, and I know there is actually a lot going on there. You may not know that happiness is not equal to freedom, perhaps you never really thought about it, or just assumed happiness is what freedom feels like.

And I know there are rather conflicting storylines in many awake, very clear teachings. One very common pointer goes something like this:

You are not your mind, you are not your body, you are not your pain.

It's a "not this, not that" no approach.

But here I am—I say yes! Truth . . . Yes, be aware of your mind (or what I call the loop); yes, be aware of your body; yes, be aware of your pain! Yes this, yes that . . .

Which intuitively feels like this great relief, because you have a direct experience of mind, of body, of pain . . . and it feels like freedom to simply let it be.

I understand the confusion. No . . . *yes.*

But actually, the "No, not your body" and the "Yes, yes, your body" are ultimately pointing to the same place. Different pathways, but the same landing place. One is pointing to "One," and the other is pointing to "One."

Like the old koan: One plus One is One.

When a person dies, or wakes up, what you get is this amazing stillness and silence that is very, very hard to express and hang words on. But words like *"You are not your body, not your mind"* seem to kinda fit.

And for about ten thousand years the old Zen boys, and others, used these words.

But these words have some innate and challenging limitations.

Yes! is a very practical approach. A very direct approach. And a direct, practical approach fits our contemporary culture, and mindset.

And ultimately it gets discovered that even if you find the place that there is "no mind, no body, no pain," the mind, body, and pain come back. One does not hang out in formlessness very long. The body, the mind, the pain return because that's what God is doing here, forming into bodies, and minds, and personalities, and worlds, and so on. Being God also means being a body, a mind, a personality. Which is part of the major pothole in the "Not your body" pointer.

I stand for yes, because it is both the start and end place. Yes embraces form and formless. It's what God is saying to you. It's what God is as you. And ultimately, what I care about is that, every moment, you embody your full authentic self. Awake to your true nature or not. And more to the point, you will not experience your full freedom until you *do* embody that yes. You are not free—and what I call *sane*—until you experience a full, deep yes to all that you are. All that you are, not just spirit, not just the vast emptiness of all the universe or all the "good"qualities. Yes, spirit, but also yes body, yes mind, yes cheeseburger and soda craving, yes sloth that doesn't get off the couch on Saturday even though it's sunny outside. Yes to longing for approval from everyone. Yes to the feelings of resentment because you can't take another minute of your boss, or your landlord, or your bank manager's bullshit. Yes. Yes to it all!

Sure, perhaps you notice you can function better when you repress some stuff, and perhaps you have found more peace since you practice some emotional control. But I am talking about freedom. I am talking about being a free human. Freedom is in the yes. A deep bow of full acceptance to everything that arises in you. Acceptance—not necessarily expression. Even though I say, "let it be," I don't mean, "verbally express the hell out of everything that moves in you," or "go fulfill every craving and urge you have." I mean a deep bow. I mean an awareness and warm welcome to what is moving. There is nothing but yes in existence. And that is a primary position to take in emancipating our conditioned insanity. It's a conditioning of insanity that represses, controls, avoids. Existence doesn't do this.

And sanity is doable. You can have more than just a little bit of peace once in a while. You can have more than an easier, more functional life. You can be free, you can be sane, you can even be fulfilled.

So ask yourself: is that what you really want?

The Quickest Route to God I Can Give You

Freedom is right here. Right now. You just need say yes. You need to be aware, and then feel a willingness and acceptance for everything that shows up in that awareness. That is a primary step to undoing the insanity. Then comes healing and authentic expression, but awareness and full acceptance are the primary steps, are the foundation.

But will you?

I promise, sanity is right here. And I do it with folks all day long. Once you get to that place of just saying yes. . . BAM! On the road to sanity, of experiencing freedom.

So the question is, can you stop and feel the intimacy of this moment? Can you feel what is arising inside of you? Can you feel that you are absolutely capable of accepting what is arising? Can you feel the perfection of the imperfection? Will you actually take it in? Because it's right here.

Can you stop for a moment and take it in? Move your attention down to your heart, take three deep breaths, and just for a second, just right now . . . feel that anything that is arising for you, in this moment, is fine. Is a-okay.

All the forms of life—and that includes you—are never very far from the source of all life, from stillness, from vastness, from love. Your job: receive it. Receive yourself, all of yourself. How do you receive it? Say yes! And then *be* yes. Be the willingness, the acceptance of everything that arises in you. It's totally doable.

Welcome every movement inside of you—I will say that again, INSIDE of you. (I'm not so interested in the acceptance of things outside of you).

So inside, your feelings, your emotions, your repressed hurts, your drives, your desires: 100 percent welcome, 100 percent of the time. Welcome. God is not in the habit of excluding anything. There is no ground to resist what arises this very moment. Only the conditioning of insanity is resisting and avoiding.

Welcome desire when it arises. Welcome pain when it arises, and every other movement that arises inside you. How many of you do that? How hard does that sound to you? Is it making you feel unsure and doubtful, or perhaps really scared that you won't be able to control yourself? Does it actually sound kinda crazy? A bit insane? We are so conditioned to insanity, that sanity seems crazy! But I ask you, how many times do you just simply welcome every single bit of *you*?

That is where peace lives. Even in pain, you can have peace, but it comes from the deep acceptance. The deep bow of yes. The deep alignment with existence. Then peace is right here.

There is a whole lot of self-rejection going on. There are years and years of conditioning that says no to all the internal movements of you. That *no* is pure vast energy suddenly becoming jammed, repressed dense energy. Pain.

How's that been working out for you?

Fulfilled?

And the mind is so conditioned, it's going to resist this. It's going to point to war (or abuse or global warming) and say, how can that be accepted? "No, there is right and there is wrong, and I will keep vigilant. I will keep myself from falling into the wrong path, because war is not welcome! And sometimes I just gotta police myself. We gotta police each other."

And I say, how is that working out for you? I say war is the product of all that internal policing. War is an external manifestation of billions of folks resisting themselves, and attacking themselves. A persecution internally looks like war externally.

How's that been working out for us?

You just have to be willing to finally say yes, to finally receive yourself. Receive every movement right now, with no story of how it needs to look. Or what you should feel. Just you. Just you, right now. I promise, this is the path to sanity; this is a primary tool to find your way back into alignment. Stop trying to not experience what you are experiencing, and instead bow in love to whatever arises. Just receive it, and then keep on receiving every bit.

And tell me how that works out for you.

For the next seven days accept every single thing, 100 percent, everything that arises inside of you, no matter what. And then let me know how it goes . . .

"I Hate You, I Hate You, I Hate You!"

I know to many of you, accepting everything that arises sounds really risky. Do I really want to do that?! How do I do that?!

It takes courage, the courage to allow, accept, and bless all of our woundedness. Courage—meaning "from the heart"—to say yes to the fear, the rage, the grief, the fight, the heartbreak, the disappointment, the temper tantrums, the depression, the selfishness, the compulsions. I know you have been conditioned to reject these parts of yourself.

However, there is a deep intelligence about your being— every part of your being. The mind gets such a bad rap, mostly because it can be wildly trance-inducing, and it can be very painful. But honestly, when the mind is in such a flap, it's usually because there is repressed pain fueling it. Really aggressive painful thoughts, when you can't seem to turn your mind off, are being fueled by repressed emotion; repressed emotion is being fueled by a repressed trauma in your system. A wound, some kind of anguish, torture, hurt, or an *owie*, as I like to call it. Owies happen. Some event transpires and we are harmed by the scenario, and we don't always have the space, ability, or know-how to process this pain fully, thus it sticks around, repressed, stuck in the body, causing all kinds of commotion.

So, I want to suggest we have a little respect for ourselves, for this gorgeous expression of Godliness called you, perfectly arising, even with your owies creating commotions all over the place.

I am in this curious position where loads and loads of these active and alive owies come to heal or process through me. Yup, not just fear, not just that one night in Edinburgh, but all the time and all sorts of pain, from all over, and all over many ages. My owies, your owies, everybody's owies come knocking on my door, surging through this body-mind. I call it the downside of oneness. And consequently, I get to see how a lot of stuff is really going down. I get to see how amazing and worthy of respect the whole story of you is. While you are busy repressing and avoiding that pain, the whole story is revealing itself to me.

For example, I have this owie, and the emotional field around it is a huge amount of rage, tons of rage—sometimes so acute it hurts like hell. It tells me that it's "super rage," the "biggest rage of all time." And sometimes that is hard to live with. So I take a lot of downtime, and I bring a tenderness to touch this raw pain, and transform it. It would be really easy for me to say, "I don't want this" or, "There is something wrong with me!" Or I suspect some of you may consider: "If I were awake enough, truly enlightened, or had 'higher' levels of consciousness, I wouldn't be like this. I wouldn't be feeling this." Yes? Sound like your mind?

But when I get down to the roots of it, something important can be seen. Of course, I can not get to the roots and see anything if I'm committed to repression and deeply involved with the avoidance. Its only because of a deep acceptance, a warm welcome, that I can actually see what's going on. So, I can see there is a wound, a painful event—well, a number of events, say hundreds of events—that could not be processed. Healing was not available, so the hurt was repressed in my body, and my body-mind created an armoring to shield all these tucked away aches. The shield gets built to protect from this raw pain. This is what is sometimes called ego, and is the source of all the repression, resistance and avoidance. It's on the firing line all the time, but it's really just a protective mechanism, but a protection you don't actually need. My shield around this huge rage sounds like this: "I hate you, I hate this, I hate everyone." When I was a child and a lot of the violence was going down, I used to scream "I hate you, I hate you, I hate you . . . fuck shit poo!" My system made these thoughts to armor from the excruciating pain tucked away in my little body. I had a violent history, lots of memory of trauma and crazy events. So my amazing system created an enemy, an enemy to save me from pain that could not be processed. My system set up: "I hate these people; I hate them so much I want to kill them." "Super rage." That's the core story from the pain, from the residual wounds. That is the sound of the armor that was set up to "protect" me from the wound. And I can bow to that shield and I can profoundly bow to the pain; I can bring immense compassion and love to all this. And ultimately, it's that love and compassion that will crack the armor and begin to heal and transform the pain.

Ironically, this willingness, this yes, this feeling that when rage shows up it's 100 percent welcome, 100 percent of the time, allows us to dissolve the armoring, and move forward without creating more of this shielding. This rage is welcome to live here—not as a mental practice, but as a genuine, heartfelt yes. This helps to transform it. The mind thinks that if you let the rage be here, if you are willing to accept rage when it shows up, it will be indulged. The mind fears that rage will become huge and become such a massive expression, that "super rage" will explode and take control, and you will suddenly be your own version of war, puking rage all over the place. And then all the neighbors will point to your rage and comment about what a huge ego you have . . . that you're really caught in egoic behavior!

Nope. It's actually repression that does that. Repression creates the ego, repression maintains an ego, and repression hits a max level and then explodes when you are looking the other way, running from it, or trying to push it down further. The pressure of repression creates the ultimately futile shielding and the subsequent explosion. And boy, do I know a lot about that!

Direct experience will show you the difference. Direct experience will show you that when you say yes, be yes, be compassionately loving and meet whatever is arising, whatever is arising will transform and eventually take its natural place in your system, coming home to rest.

There is a huge amount of intelligence working for you. A little respect for yourself will bring you a lot closer to understanding that whatever arises is not a problem to be repressed or avoided. Feelings arise for very intelligent reasons, even if the little tool called mind cannot know why.

I'm not advocating a practice here, folks. I am showing you how to embody the truth of your being, your whole being. We can afford to be inclusive with ourselves, even with resistance. Let us find the courage to accept, allow, and bless whatever arises. This is the quickest route to God that I can give you. I know it may sound overly simple, but God is simple. That is the thing. God is so simply right here. Freedom is right here at the gates of a tender, loving yes to everything that is you.

A Simple Welcome to the Many Shapes of God

Yes to everything. Existence has no problem with any of it. We don't need to have a problem with it. Yes. It's not a mental activity, or a new technique. It's not a contrived yes, but a yes that comes from your heart. Existence's yes. A yes that welcomes even your deepest no. Yes to heartache, yes to frustration, yes to pain, yes to this discomfort between the ribs, yes to the tears, yes to the ache, yes to the anger, yes to the rant about how careless and uncommunicative and what mean, selfish people there are . . .

Even a simple yes to the stories. The stories can get very seductive, and before long you're entranced with the details and identified within the story. *yes* helps you to stay clear of the pain of detailing every circumstances. Just a simple yes.

Today it takes a form of grief. YES.

Yes, to how sad I am, even yes to wanting to have better ways to protect myself, yes to the me who wants to avoid broken hearts and mean people. Yes. Yes.

Yup, sad. Yup, broken heart. Yes I don't want to be in pain, yes.

Yes to everything that arises. Not as a process to solve anything, but as a simple welcome to the many shapes of God.

It takes courage to embrace the fear, the pain, the disappointment, the heartbreak, as we would embrace joy, a smile, or sunshine on a spring day. Those are easy to welcome. Only when there is no resistance—even to resistance—can you know freedom, the whole freedom of God Only then will you understand directly that there is nothing wrong with you.

Evan: It Doesn't Feel Like It's Enough to Just Accept This.

Evan: There is a feeling of being unworthy, and I can feel a knot of physical pain in my gut. This pain is here and this feeling, so there must be something wrong. It's not complete to just accept this. Spiritually, I can't help but have the idea that there is a more fluid way to live.

Kiran: There is reality. In reality you notice a knot in your gut and feelings of being unworthy, but there is no future moment. A future in which you don't have this pain. That is a story being tagged on, a "one day you will arrive" story. There is just this moment. And this moment contains a physical pain, and a feeling of unworthiness. In this moment you are also free. You are freedom itself, and this includes freedom to be aware of pain and feelings.

Yes, but I feel this hook: as long as I have this pain, I'm not free. Something is incomplete. That just feels true.

We know this moment contains pain and feelings. Pain and feelings that you may attend to. The filter or belief—that you want to live in a more fluid way, or that pain needs to be overcome —is not truth, it's *intention*. I can hold this intention with you that the pain will resolve, but I don't know that it will. It's also not true that one day you will be complete, or free when pain and bad feelings doesn't arise. This is all a story, and perhaps a misunderstanding that freedom means no pain and no feelings . . . but freedom is inclusive, not exclusive.

So what do I do with this pain? It doesn't feel like freedom.

This may sound overly simple, or hard to take in, because "I am not free" has an opposite lie attached to it. The opposite is "one day I will be free." The freedom that you are right now, your freedom, is *inclusive*, you will feel it when you're free to simply feel the pain. Even if you believe you are broken, you are still free, but projecting this broken story. This broken story is nothing but a conditioned, habitual response, filtering your experience of life. And then when you stop resisting the pain and feelings that arise . . . that which you are pointing to as proof of your "brokenness" and simply allow it to be here, welcome it, you will begin to hear what the pain is telling you and how you can attend to it. And that is how you start to find that more fluid way to live.

Okay, I get it . . .

three

Alchemy

Alchemy: to transform. Transforming pain into love, and from love back into the vast silence of all creation.

Alchemy is dissolving pain into bliss. Pain is a dense form of energy. You can feel it; you can feel the density of pain. This density is part of why it's so painful. Love and silence are more effortless forms of energy. You can feel that too—you can feel the effortlessness of love. All things in nature move toward the most effortless path. So, you can dissolve your pain into bliss. I promise you, it's not crazy talk. It's not even hard. It's your nature, and I mean that very literally.

Tenderness Is the Strongest Force in the Universe

When the vast silence of the universe moves into form, it comes into conditioning; silence is conditioned into forms. And that conditioning is not always sane. As you may have noticed, it can be wildly insane. It can get very convoluted and distorted, and complicated and very painful.

That pain needs to be healed, the distortion needs clarity, the convolution needs to move closer toward its effortless source. That is how insanity becomes sane. To feel and live the peace, love, and bliss of our true nature. Please note that this is not a necessary step to awakening. Not at all; you can come to know God very well but have lots of insanity running. But to embody God, to embody sanity, you will need to heal. The myth is that awakening, or seeing God, will automatically make it all instantly healed, make all aspects of your life instantly sane. This is of course a myth, mostly, although lots of insanity can be blown out with a big explosive awakening. Some very rare folks have very, very little insanity to begin with, so almost nothing needs to heal—those rare "karmic-light" folk. But 99 percent of the time, there is a lot of healing needed. Not a psychological healing, but actual transformation, actual alchemy, the actual movement where pain returns back to source, back to stillness and bliss.

When insanity moves toward sanity, it's usually a process of unwinding. This kind of healing is transforming something that is dense and effortful into something light and effortless. The internal pieces—usually emotional intensity and pain—need to be seen and accepted, and then touched, in order to unwind. As well, pathways need to be recreated and reshaped externally, mapping new processes to get your needs met in the world. For example, if you have lots of insanity in your relationships, internally you will need to heal the repressed pain and old heartbreaks. And externally, a pathway will need to be pointed out. You might need to map what a healthy courtship, dating process, and relationship look like. A great coach, or mentor—someone with very sane awareness of how to date and relate, how to communicate intimately, and so on—can help you map the process of how to do this. As I like to say, there is no musculature for the sane pathway; all the muscle got built around the insane way. So even when the internal pain begins to heal, and you feel fairly sane inside, externally you will still move toward a path of insanity, because it's such a strong habitual pattern. And let me tell you from experience, that is pure hell, to be sane but still gravitationally pulled into insane pathways. Pure hell.

So how do we do this?

How do we alchemize our internal pain?

With awareness—awareness that the pain is here. Then, with a deep yes, a full acceptance of it. A full willingness to notice how it moves, what it says, what the pain feels like, all the information you can get by a warmly welcoming and seeing it. And then thirdly, with the touch of compassion, with tenderness. Tenderness is actually the strongest force in the universe. I know that sounds crazy, but it's true. Tenderness is the strongest force in the universe. Nothing can withstand it; everything crumbles before it.

One touch of true tenderness and all else crumbles. Did you know that? It doesn't matter what it is, or how big it is, or how dense it is, how loud it is, how painful it is, how old it is—tenderness will end it.

Tenderness is not so much what you do, or what someone does to you, although that is very nice. Rather, tenderness is what you already are. It's your basic nature. Being tender is being willing to surrender to your most basic nature. Tenderness is here already, and we can invite that tender part of our hearts to open. The thing about true tenderness is that it's all around us, and it's always available. It's the basic nature of all reality, the basic nature of your own humanity, and it's fully available. It doesn't always look the way the mind "thinks" it will look. But the direct experience of your tender heart is the tell-all. It's who you are at your very roots. It's worth saying again: tenderness is something *you are*, and something that, once you let your guard down, will naturally spill out of you.

We Have to Directly Face Our Own Pain

The world is benevolent in its most basic elements. The world is made of tenderness. How crazy does that sound? That may not be your conscious experience, but from the very, very roots—vast space, electrons and protons, magnetically loving each other, moving to create all the forms of the universe— that tenderness is always fully available to you. Tenderness can touch you, if you would let it in. If you let your guard down, let the armor soften, tenderness is available for you to transform your pain. Tenderness will dissolve the pain right into oblivion with one true touch.

So, how do you touch it?

More to the point, how are you avoiding it? How are you resisting all the tenderness of your most basic nature?

Because I know there is resistance. I know it so well. I know it because I am one of the best resisters out there.

I have a tremendous amount of energy, in some circles it's called kundalini, a very rapid, intense energy moving in my system all the time, rebuilding my physiological structures. I often say: kundalini can be a bitch. A few months ago my heart chakra was exploding. Not for the first time, mind you, but messy all the same. So it was a big wipeout week—no sleep, no eating, my organs twisting themselves free of misalignment and ancient turmoil. But the actual tragedy with the whole scenario was my constant wish for it to be over, my resistance. My plea for it to be something, anything different! Like sleeping and eating and getting to the garden, or working or making love. . . something other than this pain!

At first, it's just a kind of background buzz, but it gains volume as the hours pass and my enthusiasm for twisted guts wanes. I have many numerous and believable rants about poor me, about how nobody else has quite so much to deal with as me, and when the hell do I get MINE. And the real pain for me, personally, is when those rants eventually spin so much that they land and hook my attention. Because then, I suddenly believe them, and I begin to resist. And I am really good at resisting. I am a great fighter. Remember my "super rage"—it loves to get in on the action. And funny enough, this is the only tragedy. Regardless of what is going on, it's actually fine, regardless of how messy, how painful, how blustery. It's fine, until that voice, ever so subtle, comes in to evaluate the situation, and tries to pull away or control it. That's resistance. And more to the point, the resistance is the hardship. All that movement is fine until the resistance shows up. And resistance wins ground so quickly. It's so darn believable, because it has such a great mission. The mission is to distract from the pain, from the situation, from the discomfort. Resistance's main job: pull away from the pain. That's what forty thousand years of conditioning gives us.

But the truth is, the pain is part of what will set us free eventually. If we lean *into* the pain, open up to the tenderness of our souls, walk right into the heart of the issue with the beam of compassion and sweet, sweet tenderness—there is the transformation. It's pure alchemy. Yup, that's where it is . . . right in the heart of the pain. It's the only place where the solution is. But to get there, you have to meet resistance and that's the part that can be a challenge.

I was on the phone with a friend recently, and his resistance sounded like: "What can I do to avoid this suffering . . . where did I go wrong?" Yeah, I know that one too. Sounds so sane, right? So believable! Almost impossible to detect, but still, that is the voice of resistance; that is the only thing here that is creating the suffering. Suffering in actuality is the resistance to the pain, resistance to what is going on in you. That is what suffering is. In my life, it's usually an intense episode of kundalini that sparks the resistance, but it can be any number of pains that will trigger the "nope, I don't want this going on" feeling. But whatever the pain, the solution is when you bravely and directly move right into the heart of your own discomfort, grief, anger, etc. And to do that, you will have to hurdle over the resistance. Sometimes that is impossible, so then you have to meet the resistance tenderly. We have to directly face our own pain with tenderness. That's the only place where healing is. The good news is that regardless of how good you are at fighting everything, eventually the resistance is going to be futile, and you will face the pain, and you will find that's the beginning place. Right there, right in the very place you have avoided.

Awareness Can Be Very Potent When Used Correctly

I like the word *karma*. I like that it can mean some baggage right now, and baggage with a past. I like the word *pain-body* too—such a great descriptive term from Eckhart Tolle.

This is what I know about dissolving pain, what I refer to as *karmic pain-bodies*.

First off, when we suffer or are in the sudden grip of an owie, be it a rage, a grief, an anxiety attack, a panic attack, an attack of resistance, anything really that just feels awful, feels like pain—that is a pain-body. But I like to say *karmic pain,* because although it's showing up right now, in this moment, it has a big past. It has a historical perspective. For instance, your heart is breaking right now because your sweetheart is packing up and leaving, but that pain also feels like when your high school crush moved away, and that also feels a lot like when you were eight and your dog Sammy died, and so on. You get what I am saying here. So, as I like to say, karmic pain. And there are actually three layers to that pain. The first layer is up at the top of your body, in the head. The voice in your head yap, yap, yapping away. You will recognize it. You know it well, a seemingly endless stream of irritated thinking. (You can only imagine what my beloved "super rage" has to say about things.) It can also take the form of trancing out of the present moment. Trancing out of some painful thoughts by getting fuzzy and distracted, feeling foggy, and even erecting a fragile and artificially happy mood.

Then there is a second layer. If you were to imagine a cord dangling down from that chatty thought stream, or trance, and follow it down, down, you would discover an emotional field, perhaps say grief, or rage, or anxiety, panic, depression—anything that contains fear and unhappiness. That is the emotional field of the pain body. That is the emotional radiance of those voices ranting away in your head.

Then follow the cord down to the third layer, a physical sensation. Usually it feels like a muscle knot, but a knot in some very hard-to-reach part of your body. Usually you can feel it behind your heart, or solar plexus, in your ribcage, in your throat, but really it can be located anywhere. Regardless, you can feel it, and it won't take much to notice that particularly vibrating ache, like a stone in your chest, or a dull ache, or an acute stab. Super rage was an acute throbbing that lived in my right side, under the ribcage.

So here is the trick: stay with the physical sensation. Bring your awareness solely to the sensation, like you can be aware of your breath if I ask you to do that . . . a soft kind of listening. Awareness can be very potent when used correctly. But you can't approach this with the intention to get rid of the pain. It has to be an intention to finally welcome and unearth the sensation from its life of repression, an intention to finally see what is going on, to accept and love this pain. It will be all for naught with the wrong intention, a fruitless endeavor. So, very closely, like your awareness were touching it, holding it, focus on that physical knot. Be aware of touching it, not at the distance of an observation, but as the intimate sensation of touch. The tenderness of your very nature, tenderly holding the painful sensation. Like it was a child or animal in pain, hold this pain with your tender awareness.

Now simply stay there, unwavering and unmoving. Like our beautiful Zen brothers and sisters have taught us, by sitting totally unmoved at the wall. Stay with your awareness touching that physical sensation, unmoving. Regardless of the emotional story, which will get very big and try to grab your awareness, or your thoughts, which will get very seductive and strategic; for example, "This is so stupid" or "I have to remember where I put that message from work" or "Did I forget to turn off the stove?" And the best, "I think this is making it worse; am I just making this worse? It didn't feel so bad before." Regardless of the thoughts brewing up a storm, stay put. Simply stay with the one act of touching the physical sensation.

If you drift away, simply come back to the sensation of the physical knot. Stay there and you will notice . . . perhaps it takes a couple of minutes, perhaps much less, but you will notice that the physical sensation will begin to dissolve. And the dissolve will feel delicious, like when a muscle knot deliciously unwinds during a massage. Don't confuse this with the sudden disappearance of the sensation that can often come with resistance. When pain has been conditioned for a lifetime to hide and be suppressed, it can do funny things when we put awareness directly on it. When we finally say yes, and then go touch it with tenderness, it can disappear suddenly or jump around; these are further attempts to stay hidden and repressed. Should this happen, it's okay; you know where that knot of pain really is. After all, it's been aching away in the background your whole life. Just keep your tender touch on that spot, and eventually the disappearing will subside, and the full painful ache will reveal itself; then it will surrender to the tender touch of awareness. When you get that unmovable touch of pure tender awareness, it will just take a couple of breaths, and the physical pain will unwind. And with it, the emotional field and the irritated thought stream, or foggy trance. It will all dissolve permanently. If it feels very persistent, likely that is an area where there are a ton of karmic pain bodies hanging out. But it will dissolve, that pain, that ache, will dissolve and be transformed into a much more comfortable ease.

Karmic pain can be undone. You may have heard otherwise . . . so don't take my word for it. Directly experience it yourself, channel your inner Zen dude, and try it out.

Big Karmic Pain in the Ass

And once that knot dissolves, and the yummy relief is felt, you may notice several more knots rising up to be dissolved. I won't lie to you, it can become addictive: busting up the knots, dissolving the emotional field, ending the wicked rant going on in your head. Yup, it's awesome. It's amazing to realize you can heal. That you—and by you I mean every one of us—is a healer. We can heal. Our basic nature is a healing salve. Innate in us is the ability to heal. It's just insane conditioning that has pulled us away from our natural ability to heal pain. And just so you know, it's totally fine to start doing it all the time. In the middle of the night, when a pain body or rant wakes you up out of a dead sleep, it's okay to do it there too. After a while, you will notice a considerable amount of peace and ease where you used to panic, fear, worry, and fret.

It's not without discomfort. Yup, it can be a heck of a lot of discomfort busting up some of the big knots. But actual transformation is available. It's tricky not to get lost in the emotional field. Stick with the physical sensation; don't waver from the physical place. In the middle of the process, it can seem bigger and louder and more insurmountable, and that's when you know you're at the peak of your descent into dissolving. It's darkest just before dawn, as they say. You can get help: a guided meditation, or a teacher talking about stillness, a teacher with a lot of awareness. Play the recording or video and get saturated in the stillness. Keep it playing in the background for help.

And also worth mentioning: busting up karma is not "in order to" get closer to God or anything—it's a solution to the big karmic pain-in-the-ass! You can get real, real close to God messed up just as you are. Being free, embodying your freedom, however, must include healing. And it is possible to heal your pain and insanity, without awakening to God. You have the innate ability. You can end your deep, ages-old suffering. Those horrific patterns don't have to hang about.

You may have noticed there is another way to bust up the karma: by living a total chaotic mess. Sometimes you just can't catch the suffering until it's in midstream and you are about to punch out the man in the parking lot for taking your spot. Okay, so that too can happen. And it's very painful. It's a strange and awkward thing we humans have going on. For some reason, sometimes life has to get unbearably painful for us. And how much pain a human can endure seems almost endless. It can get real, real bad up in there before the alarm goes off and change becomes the next and only option. I wish it were otherwise; I truly wish we all understood that fear and pain can push you toward an evolution, but that vision and joy—what I like to call *joy-body*—can inspire. Imagine if us humans just needed inspiration to make change; imagine if joy could motivate us enough to drop the beliefs that are so painful, and try a different way. But we're not there yet. So, the other way you get to burn out your karmic pain is to simply live it. The big karmic wipeout. So if you, or your buddy, seem to be caught in some endless pattern of pain, be gentle. It's still the primary operating system we have going on. Eventually it's going to get so bad, it will stop. I know it's hard to watch, but c'mon—we've all been there.

What the Suicidal Impulse Actually Is

In terms of healing pain with tenderness, I also want to include suicide. Don't you think it's odd that so many folks want to escape, want not to be here anymore, or want to kill themselves, even after tons of satsang or dharma talks? You may not have noticed this, but I notice things like this. I don't know why it has to be so taboo to talk about it. Most of us imagine suicide at some point—usually when we are teenagers. Some of us know people who have committed suicide, we consider it, we wonder about it . . . and why wouldn't we?

But I want to mention that those very real considerations, those very real suicidal impulses, are conditioning, are a very specific kind of programming in the system.

I know a lot about this, because my body was full of this programing. I had no idea until I woke up. And, well, there were a couple of years in there, post-awakening, that I had to struggle not to throw myself off the twenty-second-story balcony of my apartment. Some days all I could do was breathe and try to not throw myself off the balcony. But having been there, and because I primarily see things at the quantum level, I can shed a lot of light on the subject.

So let me tell you, and then you can tell others, what suicide actually is. I'm very passionate about getting the word out, so I am going to ask you to help me do this.

As I mentioned, our pain, our karmic pain body, has three layers. One of those layers is an emotional field. And to be accurate here, at the quantum level, imbedded in that field is a programming. A code, if you will. A code that will activate when necessary. There is a grand system of protection at work for ourselves. It represses or blocks pain that is perceived to be beyond our seeming ability to process it (whether that is true or not is actually up for grabs.) Regardless, this is the message—"I cannot take this pain"—and the pain gets tucked away for a later day, presumably when we have the space and ability to process it. And an emotional field grows around this owie. Then every time something, someone, or some life event reminds us of this pain, or "triggers" us, we feel a jab from this emotional field.

So the impulse of suicide is programming, is a code, a byte of information planted inside the emotional field of this pain. The code basically reads: "Under no circumstances is this pain to be felt or experienced. Everything that can be done to avoid feeling this pain will be done. Even if we have to terminate the organism, we will prevent this pain from emerging."

That is the programming. And interestingly enough, the programming itself occurs somewhat randomly. If you actually unearth a pain, or owie—either through touching it with your tenderness, or by reliving the pain—you will see that some enormously painful owies don't have suicidal programming in their emotional field. For example, when your uncle molested you when you were twelve: no suicide programming. However, the owie from when you were five and not allowed to wear your favorite green shirt: there is it, suicide code. It's very random.

Real suicidal impulses are simply this programming at work.

So know this: It's just some random, primal coding in the system. See it for what it is; then ignore the coding, ignore the impulse. See it for what it is, just some random code, and then go forth through that emotional field into the physical layer to dissolve the pain and get healing.

And please, let's all talk about this. Let's share the details of this suicide code. Perhaps if we can acknowledge that it's natural to talk about death, and that considering death is just as normal as considering birth, we can begin to heal it.

It's also worth noting that when we get still, quiet, and contemplative—say, like after ten hours of dharma talks—often pain can begin to surface, repressed emotions can begin to surface, and up comes the random suicide programming with it. We might all be lucky like that, I guess. Nevertheless, don't get all involved with it; just know it's part of the coding of the pain, and get to the physical sensation where your tenderness can touch it, and help dissolve it.

Joe: The Knot of Pain Feels Huge and Unmovable.

*Joe: There is such a big knot, like a big rock, in my chest. I can't seem to penetrate it. I just want to avoid it, and now I can't seem to **not** notice it. It's surprising to me. I think I have always felt it.*

Kiran: Okay, lets try something . . .Can you imagine your stepdaughter, when she was a baby? This nurturing love is the tenderness that is needed. It's available. Please imagine her lovely baby hands and smile, and that tender baby affection. Brew this up in your system. Get a strong dose of your tender, loving, nourishing self. As many details of her as a baby that will draw a very strong sense of love in you. Take some time with it. Really get those feelings activated. Now transfer that image to the rock in your chest. Imagine that rock is your child. It may take a moment for the rock to soften, but this nourishing touch will begin to soften it. Play with your imagination, imaging all kinds of details to access that very sweet, loving touch. Let your love for your daughter be the same love and tenderness that touches this rock in your chest. Let your love for her be a mirror of the love you have for your own pain. Love yourself as you would love your own child if she was in pain.

Yes, I can feel that.

Good. Stay with that for a while. Let's sit here for five minutes doing this.

I feel an emotional upswell. I feel angry, upset, and I can feel this pain, this rock, very intensely, like an aggressive shock of pain in my chest.

Yes, that anger and upset is the pain inside of the rock. And when it unwinds, the pain will be released, and the emotional field will dissolve.

I didn't know I could touch it. It feels like such a relief to hold this pain. Like it's okay to hold it. I like this feeling. It's suddenly not so painful, or so loud. It's a relief. It's very touching—emotionally, I mean, like maybe I've been wanting this for a long time.

Yes, stick with the physical sensations. As the rock begins to soften, it will crack open, unwinding a traumatic experience or story. That can be very intense, and hard to not get swept up in. Stay with the physical sensation, pouring love and light on it, touching it , but not getting distracted away from it.

four

Alignment

Alignment is authenticity in action. Saying, and standing in, what is true for you. Being what you are. Being and speaking and embodying all that you are. There are no "shoulds" or "ought tos" in alignment. There is only a feeling of truth; an internal gauge of what's true, and only true for you, that has the sweetest essence of right action even though you have no idea why. That is alignment. And like the other tools, it's actually very, very available.

If You Can't Find It, It's Not a Yes

As I have mentioned, the vast, empty spaciousness of all creation has movement; that movement is love. And that love can take the form of what we call *desire*. Desire has two faces. One is love, a song, a calling for more love, more joy, more forms to experience; this is life moving with very little distortion. To us, this type of desire feels like wishing. It has a light feeling; it has an inspired feeling. It feels like what I call a "delicious yes." When I teach, I talk about listening for those yummy, delicious yes feelings. I like that term because you can sense the feeling, listening for the activity or choice that feels so yummy, at the gut level. Yum, yes. Yes please, delicious.

The other face of desire is more painful. It actually is pain, a distorted dense energy that is jammed and repressed. It feels like striving, like seeking, like a stab of need that often includes a feeling of never being fulfilled, always hungry, always lonely, always missing something. These internal movements of need and lack create the primary insanity of our world. "You" don't really create your reality. Our unconscious wounds going round and round, constantly filtering and manifesting experience—that's what largely creates our reality, creates our experience of the world An economic recession is, at the level of its source, a culmination of the lack-of-wealth, or lack-of-worth, story. Hours and hours of "I don't have enough." "There is no money." "I need more." "I am worthless." "I don't matter." Thousands of hours of some kind of lack story, some kind of "I am less than" story.

You probably have a sense of how often that striving, seeking, painful stab of need story is rolling around in your head. Sometimes it's acute, sometimes it's more subtle and feels like "I should do this," or "I ought to do that," or "we should all do this." The beliefs behind those ideas: I am lacking value, or I am not capable, or I am not enough, and I will get more value, be a better person, be more loved, when I do this thing that I "should" do. How saturated are you in the story? This is the power creating your world. Unless you are blessed with a very light woundedness—karmic light—you will have unconscious pain creating many of the experiences of your life. Sorry, those of you (you and me both) with harsh pain, big owies. . .

☾

But the good news is, it doesn't have to be this way. In reality, life is very good at living itself. "You," however, are not so great at making it all happen. It's very hard for you to create everything you need to be fulfilled. But you can get in the way of letting life unfold it all. For instance, to pay the rent we can easily see there are a million small choices and events that equal that money in your hand, like getting the job, being healthy and safely arriving at the job each day, and well, a million microcosmic events; and we can call all those tiny movements "life." You couldn't imagine each microscopic event lining up, let alone create it all. From this observance, you are not the one here that is paying the rent, you're the one *trying* to pay the rent. And the irony is, trying to make it all happen actually gets in the way of it all happening effortlessly. When the distortions, effort, trying, get out of the way, life can simply take care of itself. You actually experience it all the time; for instance, when you want something to happen, but life gives you something else, and then, in hindsight, you see that something else was 100 times better! When we get out of the way, amazing opportunity can show up. We haven't been taught this- we have been taught that life is hard, life is a struggle. We see starvation, we see war, we see drought, and it re-enforces to us that life is indeed a struggle. We don't see how our insanity, our struggle is what is creating that starvation, that war, that global warming. Life is fabulous at taking care of our needs, and doing so in a way that is deeply fulfilling on so many levels. But we have to step out of the way, surrender the struggle, this "trying" mind, for life to do it. Ironically, how "you" get *out* of the way is by standing in that deep, delicious yes. I know that sounds weird, but the best way to get out of the way, is to listen to what feels like the most delicious thing to do in each moment. That's the actual expression of life simply moving without distortions of pain. Its hard to understand this, because it feels like this is exactly where your "me" is. In actuality, it's the place of "no-me." When something feels very delicious, like a deep yes, that is life whispering instructions to you of what the next step is. You cannot possibly calculate all the details that would have to line up for any circumstance to unfold... life does that. Your part in this flow is to listen for the most obvious step, what feels like the most delicious thing to do in this moment. But we have all this insane conditioning that leads us away from our natural God-given instincts.

You do not feel a lack of money because your bank account is empty. Your bank account is empty because you have deep story of not enough money, or unworthiness, or that you don't really matter. And we spend a lot of time trying to be otherwise, trying to improve our situation. But sadly, most of the things we try don't actually transform anything; they may manage a different outcome for awhile, but because they are management strategies of the "me, trying to get something," they can't create permanent transformation. But you may have noticed that already.

What *is* going to fix the situation is first healing the wound that creates the unconscious and constant lack story. Without the wound, management tools have more impact. But the simplest and most profound way to make an impact is to start standing in alignment, to start standing in your delicious yes.

Yes.

It has a vibration when it's true. We don't have to know what that is; we just feel it when it's completely true for us. You just know it. If you can't find it, it's not a yes. A yes stands out. It feels delicious. It feels like, well. . . yes. I tell folks all day long, find that delicious feeling . . . feel that? That is a very clear yes. And if you have a hard time finding that clarity, you can use this as a gauge: Is it delicious? Does it have some essence of delicious to it? If it doesn't, if it feels onerous, or hard, or obligatory, or heavy, then it's not a yes. A true yes is not you forcing everything you feel into yes, but noticing what is already a yes, naturally, uniquely, for you. This includes noticing what is *no*—for example, no way, or I don't know, or I'm not sure, or maybe, or get back to me, or let me think about it.

Because a yes just sounds like this: Yes.

Sometimes it's hard to stand in that authority, hard to lean into what we know is a yes. We get so much conditioning telling us what our yes "should" be. It gets all mixed up. We are trained to compromise our internal compass from time beyond, but it has never served, and will never serve.

If it's true, 100 percent true, for you, it's true for all beings everywhere. At the very source of all of life is Oneness. It's a Oneness game. There is only One of us here, right? So, what is yes for you is yes for the One. You don't become One; you're IT right now, in those shoes, with that hair, and those hungry, sad, tired, smiling, bored, engaged eyes . . . yes, you. Are the One.

Right?

But how in the heck does society function if we are all following our yes?!

"Good Samaritan" mind, "spiritual" mind, "fear" mind, "sheepish" mind, "parent" mind, "good spouse" mind—are all impotent attempts to stand in for the absence of your own authority, or your most aligned, right, harmonic movement. This movement is inside of your yes. But I dare you to find out for yourself. What is your yes right now? You might not be able to know what it is, or know it just in this moment, or know how all the parts of the story can possibly come together. But if you are willing to listen, you will know it when you feel it. And then stand in it, without even knowing how. Just stand in it anyway.

And the thing is, the most authentic and fantastic feeling is to embody your yes. To say it and then do it. And it is possible for every yes to come together in a majestic harmony. This is called *consensus*. This is what is possible. Your yes and everyone else's yes can fit here, in this one moment. It's always a potential possibility. The quantum field is ripe for this possibility at all times—just that most of us don't have the guts to voice our yes.

I welcome you to discover for yourself how your yes, her yes, his yes, everybody's yes can all come together. Parent's yes and baby's yes can come together. Human yes and animal yes can come together. But it starts with you, and your yes.

It's kind of shocking to watch how it turns out. It's a big reverberation of freedom. But you've got to be willing to break some rules. You gotta grow some big balls. And you cannot know what a yes is for another. Nor can we have some idea of what our yes *should* be. Otherwise, we are not going to find the real one. A "should" will kill a true yes in a millisecond. But that's the thing—the most courageous act is to find your real yes, and then stand in it. And yes doesn't always make sense, doesn't always play nice with others, doesn't always smell like a rose. Yet, if you find the courage to embody yours anyway, I promise, you will be free. I know the mind has so much to say in the other direction. But if you listen for your yes, speak your yes, and then stand in it, come what may, you will begin to feel your authentic self. You will begin to know what it means to be free.

I dare you: be the change you want to see, by radically transforming your own inner landscape of compromise and "should" and anything else standing in the way of a good, solid, unmistakable "YES!" Do it . . . ruthlessly stand steadfast in your yes. Be the full representation of you, and stand in your yes for God's sake, for my sake, for the sake of peace and freedom for all beings everywhere.

Every Word I Uttered Re-created a Hell

I remember those first few weeks of my brave new world.

I remember understanding so deeply that we, all of us, every human, are here already, here . . . in heaven. This world, right now, is heaven. And it was my conditioning that was turning it to hell. Not just my conditioning, but collective conditioning. The whole darn thing—how we get taught from infants to become kids and then adults—was a mess, and was the major screw-up that was creating this hell. We were being domesticated—and not in a good way, not in a way that functions harmoniously, in essential peace and alignment with ourselves, our community, and our society. You may have noticed how totally crazy the world is. Most of our conditioning leads us to function from total madness.

I remember walking down the street a couple of days after I died. I was watching all this madness unfolding, feeling like the only sober person in a world of crazy drunks. Newly sober . . . watching. But I didn't know how to be sane in the world, how sanity moves, how sanity interacts. I didn't know how to embody sanity. I didn't even know how to talk. It felt like every word I uttered was recreating the hell I'd learned to speak from my mistaken identity. Every time I spoke, I was creating a world, a world of old, hellish concepts and alliances. I had to learn how to talk again.

I didn't know how to articulate what was true, or how to stand in a yes. But I knew that, in order to live this gift of heaven, I had to. I had to find a way to express the truth in my heart that did not isolate or separate me from my community. And for me, my community was my Self. . . you know, the whole Oneness thing; everyone here is really my Self. It was a really big challenge for a while, trying to learn how to talk, and express what was true for me, in a kind and compassionate way. (Thank you, Marshall Rosenberg, for some tools.) And there are lots of really great communication tools out there. This is a really important skill base for living the truth, and for getting around this place in relative harmony with others. Just learning how to express what is true, what I keep referring to as an internal yes, a yes that is finally, honestly, your most delicious yes.

These days, I see it all the time: someone suddenly gets a very clear insight into reality, and then they have no words. They don't know what to say, or how to say. Language just doesn't work for a while, because it had been used as a compromise tool. It's amazing how much habitual momentum of ego shows up when we speak, how full of identity our language can be. So you have to relearn how to speak, how to speak honestly, and from the truth of your heart.

For instance, if I was on a bike ride I'd organized with a friend, and it was suddenly very true to stop and sit and be alone—and I sure needed a lot of that in those early days—I was challenged. How do I say it? How do I say it to my friend and not create a rift? How do I stand in my yes and make space for whatever it was he needed to do, his yes? I didn't have any language for truth, let alone an understanding of how to speak to find consensus. And I didn't want to always be alone, to have to choose aloneness because I didn't know how to be real with anyone; here in this heaven, forced to be alone because I didn't know how to accommodate what was true and authentic for me, alongside my friend. I only wanted to be alone if alone was a yes. I just needed some skills.

So, I found some tools and learned how to speak. This is the first, and most important, step in embodying sanity. And it's how you start to notice that this place is actually kind of heaven. (So bizarre, I know, but actually true.) Standing in your yes comes next. Standing in your yes means actually getting off the bike, and going to find a space to sit alone. That's hard too—very hard if you haven't really figured out that you are worthy and important, and that what you feel and what you need are available and essential for the harmony on this planet. Ha! Can you imagine being parented like that? Can you imagine having this kind of approval for your authentic impulses? Having parents who always gave preference to your authentic voice? Oh my God, just imagine what that would be like.

So, basically none of us know how to do this. So you have to learn how. And it takes practice. Lots of practice. And then, just when you have it, when you speak it, and go about standing in it, your community will block you. It's terribly innocent, as everyone is very conditioned. We really only know how to feel connected when we are all on the same page: "Are you tired? Shall I carry your bike? Or we can park your bike and walk, or how about we ride for one more mile and then we can all stop!" This is not consensus; this is compromise.

You have to stand up for yourself. You may feel reluctant, like you're imposing your yes on everybody. So often, the internal habit has been to compromise, because the conditioned belief is that you don't matter that much, or that your preference will create disharmony. The conditioning, the need, is to avoid conflict, avoid disharmony, avoid isolation and abandonment. But if standing in your yes creates a conflict, this conflict is essential. It's a small conflict, just a simple misunderstanding, versus the larger conflict, the actual isolation and abandonment of giving up your voice, losing your truth. This filter—the conditioning of "good social behavior," or looking for group harmony—is not helpful for actual harmony. Actual harmony is your yes. Everyone's yes in this moment is already harmonious. The thought that you need to compromise, that filter of conditioning, is actually creating a much larger disharmony. "Good social behavior" is not going to create more peace on our planet. Standing in your true, delicious yes, and noticing that there is room here for everyone's yes, is how we create peace. Stand in your yes. Your yes now. You can do this. And once you start doing it, it will feel really good. And then you are one less voice in the loving crowd, suggesting all kinds of compromise and "ought tos"—one more spot in the world where authenticity is simply allowed to shine through. It may seem like a leap of faith, but it's very quickly self-affirming that there is room for everyone's authentic movements, and that essentially, by standing in your yes, you begin to give this same gift of freedom to everyone. The freedom you give yourself makes room for others to find their freedom. Phew . . .

God Is Not Lost in Oneness

Standing in your yes doesn't mean you can't commit to anything, or that you bail on your agreements and appointments. God, if I had a dollar for every awake, practicing, or spiritual person I meet who flakes on an appointment because they were "lost in Oneness" or "being present" or "refusing to make any plans" . . .

So let's say it is possible to make plans, agreements, and appointments for the future and stand in your yes. You have to feel into the potential appointment or agreement, feel if it resonates as a yes now. If it feels like a good solid yes, it's very likely to be yes "in the future." If there's a hesitant or sketchy feeling, then it's not a yes, and not worth setting up that plan or appointment. And, if it feels like a solid yes now, but when the time comes is no longer a yes at all, then stand in that; take a moment, or whatever time you need, to figure out what your yes actually is and to find the words to compassionately say what is actually true. Then make the call. It's a skill game is all: just learning how to feel your yes, speak it, and then to stand in it. After some practice, it gets very clear what feels delicious when you're making plans. You will find this harmony for yourself. And part of the learning is sometimes making the wrong choice, saying yes, and then in hindsight seeing it was a compromise. We get direct feedback from life—feelings of effort, fatigue, and a lack of grace. Once you feel that onerous effort, you will know it wasn't a true yes. And that's okay, it's a lot of skill to learn. But if you learn it, you will see how things come together with a better, more harmonious alignment.

There is an effortless path in each moment. "You" don't have to figure out the way that everything comes together. You listen for your yes, speak it, stand in it, and then listen for the whole moment to take shape with all the other yeses. It's like a puzzle, just listening for how your piece, your yes, fits. Because it does fit. It always fits and fits so beautifully. Each moment is designed just this way, as though this were some kind of heaven. Maybe, maybe it could all be sane. This moment, every moment, is designed to be sane. And you can come into alignment with this sanity by standing up for your true yes.

The deepest truth in the universe is that everything is God. God is whole. God is the only one here. One. So if it's true for you, it's true for the One. Your true voice and action is everyone's true voice and action.

One plus One is still One.

Leslie: I Don't Know Where the Yes Is.

Leslie: I have this very important decision to make, but I am confused.

Kiran: What is confusing you?

Well, because it is important. I can move across the country for a new job with my spiritual community and my sweetheart. I have very clear, enlightened teachers suggesting to me what decision to make, which holds a lot of importance for me. And my sweetheart wants to go, probably will go, regardless. Everything there will be provided: work, housing, my spiritual community, my relationship . . .

And what does your heart want?

I would have to leave my family. Leave my family, move across the country, and sell my house. It's very confusing. I have been told for years by my teacher to have no "desires," but I just can't leave my family. If only I could find a way to accept this move, but its so hard leaving them! But with all this opportunity showing up now, I feel like moving must be the yes, because it's all here, so graciously.

Sometimes your yes is a no. Your yes doesn't have to be in what is being offered. It's what your heart is saying.

In my heart of hearts, I don't want to leave.

A no is sometimes the very yes you are looking for.

Can I say no to a spiritual authority? To what is arising right now so graciously, circumstantially? All that is being provided? And so many friends think it's a good idea?

Yes.

How can I say no? Can I say no to this gift being offered?

Yes.

Oh. I see. I can see that if I say yes to the gift, I will in essence be saying no to the God of my own heart.

Yes.

Paying attention to the heart is so sweet. I see that everything else is a choice being made for me. I see. My choice is what my heart is saying.

Epilogue

A Vast Silence Living Ordinarily, Beautifully Fulfilled

Sometimes I have these cry days where I just weep all day long. I weep at the love, and at the fight. I weep for the exhausted parents who love their kid so much, I weep for the wonderful hello kiss at the international gates of the airport, I weep for the frustrated businessman swearing at the distractedly driving teenagers. Mostly I weep from love, from being so very touched. Some days are like that for me. We are actually so loving as a species; there is actually so much love here. Love is the movement behind trying to be good, trying to matter, trying to be happy. It just overwhelms me with the beauty of it.

Today is one of those days, even as I write this. But today, I am weeping for myself. Today, I am breathtaking to myself—so much so that all I can do is weep. It didn't start out that way. It was a kinda normal, making breakfast, heading to the gym morning. Usual.

Then there I was . . . silence, running on the treadmill, listening to my music. And the weeping began . . .

A number of days just after I died, I was in a panic. It

had been long enough for me to realize this disorientation, this death, was going to be permanent. I was not getting anything back. In that life that passed, I was a bit of an athlete: first a runner, then a professional dancer and actor. So here I was, freaking out—the unknown so vast before me, so unasked for, so very scary. I was desperate to get back to my world, my life, my body, me. I was desperate to get grounded in the familiar, not in this vastness. I was so disoriented, I couldn't even feel my body. I decided if I could move, run, dance, anything, I could force my body back; and force my life back. So, silence headed for the shed where my bike was, found a weird kind of forced footing, and rode like lightning through the city. It was fifteen miles to the nearest beach. Dropping the bike on the sand, I just ran and ran across the beach, waiting helplessly for silence to turn human again, to turn back into "me." I ran the full five miles of beach until it got dark, then got back on the bike and cycled home.

At home, hours later, there was still only a strange echo of body, no form, just an energy I could call "body." So I started to dance, and danced and danced. Then my legs just gave out. My knee, to be exact, simply crumpled under the pressure of nearly 35 miles of running and biking, and then dancing. So, I landed on my ass. The broken knee couldn't be felt; there was just an energy I could faintly recognize as "pain," but from a remoteness, not a direct feeling. So, that's how the grounding actually began, the embodiment. My knee broke and I sat down. I guess I needed to sit down for a while.

I sat for nearly four years, with a busted knee, and a massive emptiness echoing through all my personal identities, and through a few of the larger world identities. All the form

I knew, busted up. I sat. I sat while it all emptied out. Though it took more than a few years, eventually I started to get up. I moved to a new city, I started to build a new community, I built a new career, and I started to find my legs in this new world of silence, formlessness, and overwhelmingly acute senses.

A Fall-on-your-Knees Upswell of Gratitude

I obviously don't have much to say about getting to silence, "awakening," as it just erupted out of the blue for me. But I do know what it is to live it, about what it actually looks like to be primarily stillness. Stillness, as life outside of the ashram, off the meditation cushion, off the mountain. To actually live it, as just some woman, some girl in some city somewhere.

And now, it's been over eight years. I can stand on these knees, and not just stand—I can run. Today, I'm on the treadmill at the gym. I just cycled ten miles and ran four. I even have some of the same old songs I used to play on my iPod. Except now, it's just silence moving, loving this movement, moving just for the sheer joy of it. A totally different expression.

And I can't stop crying, crying, and crying. I traveled a long, long way to get here. And for many years in there, there was no orientation, no idea how to live, or how to handle the pain and overwhelm and massive transformations. No idea how any of this moves from disorientation to peace and sanity. I didn't know if I could, or would, ever get up. I am so moved by this woman, by this stillness that is this woman. I am here. I have a much richer, happier, more peaceful world.

A world full of love. A love that is literally spilling out of my eyes. I am so touched by this woman and the road she has traveled, what was taken, and how much it took to rebuild. And today, I'm my biggest fan.

When I woke up many years ago, I had no context, no teacher or coach to help me navigate the very treacherous terrain that came from the big bang. Amidst the outrageous pain and kundalini, and the profound disorientation, I wanted a teacher. I wanted a guide. I searched, but found very little.

Early on, in a conversation with Adyashanti—a beautiful teacher—I was so very frustrated, scared, mad: "All the awake ones are coaching the seekers on how to wake up! No one is over here, guiding the huge mess on this end. This is where the crash landing really is, but there are no coaches over here!" I used an analogy of a baseball game, with all the coaches on the bench shouting pitching instructions, while I was behind the wheel in a NASCAR race, with no coach, and no idea how to drive. Basically, he said to me, that was going to be my job. That one day, someone would turn to me, and because I'd traveled this road, I would know how to help. And that, in that moment, there would be a fulfillment, there would even be a gratitude for this hard path. I thought he was full of shit. I didn't get it, and I didn't care. Until one day, when someone turned to me in terrible pain and confusion. And there was such a profound, humbling, fall-on-your-knees upswell of gratitude, because I could help.

So, as it turns out, years later, and at great surprise to me, he was right. It is my job. My job is to help with the healing, with the clarity, and with the loving.

I don't have a particular affinity with enlightenment. As I mentioned, I never was a spiritual person; I had no idea of awakening and no real interest, and I still don't. I know first-handedly, as many of you do, that one can have a full awakening—mind, body, and emotion—"POP," identity can completely drop away and vast emptiness become the primary experience, and still the human lives out their old, dysfunctional conditioning—addictions, power issues, sexual issues, etc. We hear about it all the time. The "awake one" has dropped all identity, so is no longer suffering, but their human embodiment does not embody its full freedom; the actual body, the cell memory, can continue dreaming karmic DNA patterns, patterns still deeply aligned to this dysfunctional programming, regardless of the vast awareness that has woken up out of the program.

Also, in a similar respect, without an awakening, without directly knowing the truth of being, without the experience of form dissolving into vast silence, one can embody an authentic, free expression of humanity. There is no enlightenment, but there is freedom. We all know people like this. My first boyfriend was a free human; a free, authentic, aligned human. No enlightenment necessary.

Essentially, I don't feel the need to decide for anyone what their endgame is. I don't want to define someone else's freedom. I don't believe that everyone here needs to become enlightened. Freedom, peace, and healing, however, is available and it's not the exclusive territory of enlightenment. My deepest inspiration is to guide and teach the path towards this, the path toward sanity. This may lead you to a deeper experience of peace and fulfillment, or a full awakening into your true nature. Either way, I can help. I had the massive spontaneous awakening, I understand what that entails. It's a big can of whoop-ass, it's more than could ever meet the eye, but it is glorious.

However, the embodiment of freedom is the same for each of us, awake or not. I spend every day moving from an effortless awareness, the same awareness that is available to each of us in every moment. If I engage my mind to stand in as more than the small problem-solving tool it is—and there is a little bit of mind left that I could engage—it's immediately exhausting. It's purely depleting, the same depleting pain that many of you know so well. So, I guide each moment in this effortlessness. I let awareness take the lead. I bring a natural and innate acceptance to what arises, as "me," as "inside my body." And I attend to what arises, either with an alchemy/healing or just a simple bit of common sense. If I feel tired, I know that is welcome, and I go take a nap. I stand in my yes; I speak it and I stand in it. And the moment I sacrifice a yes for the sake of less conflict in relationship to others, or because it's not convenient, or because I don't know how to make space for my yes, I feel pain, the pain of betrayal—the same pain you feel. A beautiful pain that ensures I do not make that choice very often.

I fully attend to what is arising and fully commit to my own unique delicious yes, and that is why I live in freedom. That same freedom that is as wildly available to you as it is to me. What I live every day, every moment, is a very effortless peace, regardless of what arises. My life looks very much like everyone else's. I work, I pay bills, I have relationships, I walk the dog and take care of the garden and make dinner and answer a hundred e-mails a day. I have backaches, I get injured, I get frustrated at silly things, and I love that, or I hate that. But I never think it's a problem, or that it should all be different, or would be better if I "did something else." I don't think that any of this is a problem, or that there is a problem with "me." I live knowing that this is all God, this is vast silence living. Living ordinarily, and beautifully fulfilled.

My job is to point out for you how to embody that same freedom right now, in this moment. I offer you these tools, tools for sanity, peace, and fulfillment in every moment of your life. That's my role. And if that freedom is towards your enlightenment, great. Or after your enlightenment, great. And if that freedom is towards you living with way less pain, right now, then great.

In the marketplace, in your marriage, in traffic, in the dentist's chair, in the pressure to pay the mortgage, in the hospital bed with a cancer growing—these are not problems because "you" are insufficient, or because life is a struggle, or because you are not aligned with God. These are the very playground of all creation. This is vast silence living. This is where freedom is: right here, in the middle of your life.

How are you going to get there?

Acknowledgements

Because One plus One is sometimes one hundred—

I had two editors for this book: my friend Jo, who did such a beautiful job, and my friend Kevin, who tirelessly demanded I articulate and define my voice to the best of my ability, and who read and reread every word with me, making room for my honesty and my clarity. My humblest gratitude to both.

A huge thank you to Kevin, to my mom and dad and brothers and sisters and precious baby nephews, for the wonderful unconditioned love regardless of all the conditions. Thanks to my Yukon family for making life bearable, to Leslie for finding her yes, to Barbara for listening and loving. Thank you Jesse, Jerilyn, Gage, Jizo, Kuma, and Treko for making coming home something so sweet. Ruth, my rock, storm after storm; Adya, for being there and for being right. Mokie Joe, holding me in his heart dark night after dark night. Neige, for saying, "Let's do this!" Bentinho, who said, "You have to do this." Jo, who said, "I'll help you do this."

And you. For reading this, and for sharing part of your light with us on this journey.

Thank you.

About the Author

Kiran is a coach and teacher. She currently lives under the beautiful and warm California sun, but originally came from the beautiful and cold north. Besides giving talks and guiding meditations, she has a private practice for personal one-on-one work, and gets to spend her days doing the work she loves. You can contact Kiran or find out about Mystic Girl in the City events at her website, www.mysticgirlinthecity.com.

Notes

Notes

Notes

Notes

Notes